The Soul's Lens
JOURNAL

BONNIE BARNESS

THE SOUL'S LENS Copyright© 2020 By Bonnie Barness. All rights reserved.

A NOTE FROM THE AUTHOR 4

LIFE REVIEW 5

SHIFT ALIGNMENT 15

THE SOUL'S PURPOSE 33

SPIRITUAL PATH 43

EXPERIENCE THE SHIFT 59

ABOUT THE AUTHOR 61

A NOTE FROM THE AUTHOR

Dear Magnificent You!

You are about to receive the keys to a greater understanding of yourself and of life. Most people see themselves as physical beings living in a physical reality In truth, we are spiritual beings, Souls, that have entered into our physical body in order to actualize our spiritual essence and to create a life that reflects our True Self. Through this process, we evolve and transform the world. When you started on your new path, you acquired great Truths and Knowledge. Since **Experiencing the SHIFT** and **Manifesting Your Dreams**, you have moved to a new level of consciousness and are thinking, seeing, and being in a completely new way. What you once thought impossible is your new reality.

You are now ready to move to another level, to **Experience the Shift,** again. The awareness gained as you move forward on your new path will allow you to see your life and yourself from the higher vantage point, perspective, of the Soul. This *SHIFT* will make it possible to connect more deeply and consistently with the spiritual energies contained within yourself and all around you. Looking through the Soul's Lens, an amazing reality will emerge and another transformation and *SHIFT* will occur.

I am excited to be here with you as you gain a greater understanding of who you truly are. There is so much that awaits you on the next step of your journey. Know that you have the strength, courage and love to embrace your exciting adventure!

With Much Respect and Admiration!

Bonnie Barness

LIFE REVIEW

> "YOUR PAST CHOICES CREATED THE LIFE YOU ARE LIVING. THE CHOICES YOU MAKE TODAY WILL CREATE THE LIFE YOU WILL HAVE."

—*EXPERIENCING THE SHIFT*
By Bonnie Barness

Now is the time. This is the moment to look at the life you have lived up to now from the vantage point of the Soul's Lens. Do you know who you truly are? Has your life been a reflection of your True Self? Have you grown and evolved on every level, physically, emotionally, mentally, spiritually? Have you been fulfilling your life's purpose?

In order to see yourself through this different lens, from a clearer, spiritual perspective, it is essential to take an honest look at yourself and the life you have led. Looking through the Soul's Lens, you are free from judgment of yourself and of others. You observe for the purpose of gaining greater knowledge in order to see how you have evolved throughout your lifetime and what you have contributed. With this greater awareness, you can choose the actions that will allow you to have more of your True Self, your Soul, reflected in the world as you go forward in life.

In the following pages, you will have the opportunity to gain clarity about what you have learned and have created through your previous actions. These insights will provide the awareness needed to actualize more of your True Self and Soul's purpose in the world as you continue your life's journey on your authentic and amazing path.

LIFE REFLECTIONS, LIFE LESSONS

What contributions have you made to individuals and to society throughout your lifetime?

_____
_____
_____

Identify parts of your life that have gone smoothly.

PERSONALLY

_____
_____

ACADEMICALLY

_____
_____

PROFESSIONALLY

_____
_____

PHYSICALLY

_____
_____

Identify parts of your life that have been very challenging.

PERSONALLY

ACADEMICALLY

PROFESSIONALLY

PHYSICALLY

NEW AWARENESS:

✎ **Major life challenges**

1.
2.
3.
4.

Have these challenges been met?

◯ YES   ◯ NO

If yes, describe how.

✎

REFLECT ON WHAT YOU HAVE LEARNED ABOUT YOURSELF AND ABOUT OTHERS THROUGH THESE EXPERIENCES.

What skills and insights have you gained?

✎

How, specifically, have you grown and evolved due to these life experiences and lessons?

✎

How have they contributed to your ability to actualize your True Self and to manifest your dreams until this moment in time?

✎

✎ Present challenges and areas of resistance.

✎ When met and moved through, how will you have evolved?
What will you have learned?

Knowing what you know now, what different choices are available that will allow for your Soul, your True Self, to be reflected in the world?

✎

Reflecting on your present relationships, choices and opportunities, which new actions do you want to take in order to actualize more of your True Self in the world?

✎

PERSONAL ASSESSMENT

HOW MUCH OF YOUR TRUE SELF IS REFLECTED IN THE VARIOUS RELATIONSHIPS IN YOUR LIFE?

Your Relationship with Family Members

Your Romantic Relationship

Your Friendships

Your Daily Interactions

HOW MUCH OF YOUR TRUE SELF IS REFLECTED IN THE VARIOUS AREAS IN YOUR LIFE

Work

Free Time

Gifts and Talents

BEING TRUE TO YOURSELF

THINK OF AN IMPORTANT DECISION YOU MADE IN YOUR LIFE.

Describe the circumstances and your decision.

_____
_____
_____
_____
_____
_____
_____
_____

ASK YOURSELF THE FOLLOWING QUESTIONS:

Was my decision based on what I thought I "should" do, due to my upbringing?

◯ YES   ◯ NO

Was my decision based on what other's would think of me?

◯ YES   ◯ NO

Did I make the decision based on being "true to myself"?

◯ YES   ◯ NO

> "THE SOUL'S PURPOSE IS TO ACTUALIZE ITSELF IN THE WORLD, TRANSFORMING ALL WITH ITS RADIANT LIGHT"

—*THE SOUL'S LENS*
By Bonnie Barness

SUPPLEMENTAL READING: *FINDING THE BALANCE…A GUIDE TO SANE LIVING* BY BONNIE BARNESS

SHIFT Actualization begins with a strong connection to your True Self. Your True Self, your Soul, is the source of your power to create. When you are in alignment, in balance, you are able to tap into this amazing source in order to actualize your True Self in the world and to manifest your dreams. Identifying the areas in which you are out-of-alignment allows you to make the adjustments and to experience the healing necessary to reconnect deeply and profoundly with your True Self.

Once you are in alignment, it is essential to live in balance throughout each and every day. Utilizing the knowledge acquired from within *"Finding the Balance: A Guide to Sane Living"* and *"Experiencing the SHIFT: A New Way of Thinking, Seeing and Being"*, will support you in staying connected to your True Self and in balance through life's ups and downs.

As you move forward on your new path, in alignment, more of your gifts and talents will become available to manifest your dreams. You will be able to access more of your True Self and spiritual energy as well. Spiritual gifts will be revealed. New information provided. Your energetic frequency will increase and with it a greater ability to fulfill your life's purpose and to experience another *SHIFT* into an even higher level of conscious awareness.

"
WHEN YOU UNDERSTAND, IT ISN'T POSSIBLE TO JUDGE. "

—*THE SOUL'S LENS*
By Bonnie Barness

KNOWING YOUR INNER CORE

List times and circumstances when you felt centered and connected to your Soul, your True Self.

CENTEREDNESS AS A PRIORITY

Describe how you feel when you are living life in balance, connected to your True Self.

Describe how you feel when you are not centered and are disconnected from your Soul, your Essence.

Describe specific actions you will take to keep unhealthy energy and people from effecting your inner peace.

Describe the actions you will take throughout the day to stay connected to your inner peace and calm.

STAYING IN BALANCE

What expectations do you have of yourself and of others that effect your sense of balance?

What can you do differently in order to stay in balance and connected to your True Self, your Higher Self?

As you go to higher levels of consciousness, do you notice a difference in your energy, your vibrational frequency?

As your energetic frequency becomes faster, what can you do to stay in balance?

Do you feel fulfilled?

◯ YES   ◯ NO

What steps will you take in order to create a deeper sense of fulfillment?

What do you need to do in order to feel a greater sense of connectedness to people, the environment, other living things and your own spirituality, to your True Self?

What actions will you take to fulfill your physical, financial, emotional, creative and spiritual needs?

How often are you critical or judgmental of yourself?

○ NEVER   ○ SOMETIMES   ○ ALWAYS

How often are you in touch with what you need?

○ NEVER   ○ SOMETIMES   ○ ALWAYS

How often do you give yourself what you need?

○ NEVER   ○ SOMETIMES   ○ ALWAYS

Do you treat others with kindness and respect?

○ NEVER   ○ SOMETIMES   ○ ALWAYS

Do you treat yourself with kindness and respect?

○ NEVER   ○ SOMETIMES   ○ ALWAYS

Are you comfortable receiving from others?

○ YES   ○ NO

Do you love yourself?

○ YES   ○ NO

Are you or someone close to you dealing with a profound loss?

○ YES   ○ NO

How can you stay connected to your True Self while dealing with painful situations that are out of your control?

What are you doing to stay connected to your True Self while feeling, expressing empathy and compassion?

TAKING ACTION

What will you start doing in order to take better care of your physical health and have more of your True Self reflected through your body?

What thoughts can you replace to create more peace and calm within?

What artistic and creative gifts do you have?

How can you begin to actualize them in the word?

Describe how it feels to be expressing the beauty of your Soul.

Describe how it feels being connected to your True Self and living in the moment, free of thoughts of the past and the future.

Reflect on how the actualization of these gifts are connected with your spiritual lessons and your Soul's purpose.

THE HIGHER SELF

Describe a recent situation in which you were connected to your True Self.

Describe a recent situation in which, in the interest of reflecting your True Self, you would have preferred to have acted differently?

What would have done differently?

Visualize yourself living life, connected to your Soul, your Higher Self. What do you see? What are you doing? What beauty are you manifesting?

Think of a past conflict when you or the other person had a need to "be right." Now replay it in your mind's eye. Notice that you are both coming from a place of wanting to understand the other rather than "being right." Describe what occurred and how this conscious interaction reflects your new way of being in the world.

Describe a situation in which your actions reflected a desire for the other person's well-being as much as for your own.

On a scale from 1 to 10, rate the frequency in which your actions are a reflection of your Higher Self, your True Self.

BEING AT CAUSE

Describe a situation in which you reacted emotionally and are now aware that your actions were not in alignment with your True Self.

Replay the same situation, this time utilizing your emotional intelligence to understand the situation more clearly. Get in touch with the feelings and thoughts you were having at the time. Consider the various actions you might have taken. Which one would most likely have created an outcome that would have better served your Higher Self.

How does the outcome differ when choosing to be '"at cause, making a decision, versus being "at effect" being reactive?

Describe a situation in which you felt a need to defend yourself. Now visualize the same situation as you utilize your Detachment Muscle to hold yourself back from doing so. From this place of observation, what do you notice internally and externally?

Spiritual alignment occurs when you have connected to your True Self and have released a lot of emotional pain. When aligned, the spiritual energies can then flow through you, free of previous energetic blockage. Please take some time to consider areas in need of healing: physically, emotionally, mentally and spiritually. Now, write down below what you have discovered.

What specific actions will you take to heal from the past in order to create inner alignment and true balance?

After going through deep healing, notice how your spiritual energies are being expressed in the world. Describe below.

PRECIOUS ENERGY

DEFINITION:

"THE ENERGY YOU HAVE AVAILABLE TO CREATE YOUR LIFE AND MANIFEST YOUR DREAM.

IT IS PRECIOUS BECAUSE IT IS YOURS.

IT IS FINITE.

YOU GET TO CHOOSE HOW YOU USE IT.

CHOOSE WISELY."

—*EXPERIENCING THE SHIFT*
By Bonnie Barness

THE SOUL'S PURPOSE

SUPPLEMENTAL READING: *MANIFESTING YOUR DREAMS* BY BONNIE BARNESS

Looking at your life through The Soul's Lens, you begin to realize that coincidences are not simply coincidences. You begin to notice that there is something greater than yourself working with you to actualize your Soul's purpose. It is important to pay attention to these occurrences in order to see if there are messages being conveyed to you.

From this higher vantage point, you may also notice how external events often appear and support the manifestation of your Soul's desire. This happens when powerful thoughts and emotions are connected to what your Soul has chosen to do during this lifetime. Notice when synchronicities occur and keep your mind open to the meaning contained in each experience.

Sometimes, your life's purpose is not what you think it will be. At times, it may be what you long for and at other times that may not be the case. As you move forward on your new path, you will gain more insight and understanding. Have patience. Much will be revealed.

Living life from a higher level of consciousness, you will no longer be setting and achieving goals. Rather, you will be living your life manifesting dreams, Manifesting is a very different process. Rather than pursuing your ego's desire, you will be listening to your True Self and noticing different spiritual forces which are waiting to guide you in fulfilling your destiny and purpose. As you utilize the powerful Manifesting Gifts and Principles contained in the *Manifesting Your Dreams Journal*, new dreams most certainly will become reality. What dream will be the next on your Manifesting Path?

What can you do that will make your life have more meaning?

What dreams have you thought of manifesting and have not yet pursued?

What do you love to do?

What are you good at? What are some of your natural gifts?

Describe a situation in which your were able to step outside of your own thoughts and emotions and look at it through the Soul's Lens.

What did you observe about yourself, others and the situation?

What actions did you choose based on this higher vantage point?

What spiritual lessons were presented to you?

What did you learn? How did you grow?

Reflect on how this situation may be related to your Soul's purpose.

What did you love doing when you were younger?

What did you really want or pursue that did not happen? What knowledge have you gained about yourself, your life, your present purpose? Do you want to pursue it now?

What new activities would you like to bring into your life?

If you could pursue any dream, what would it be?

AVENUES OF POSSIBILITIES

What have you thought of creating that you can see yourself taking action on now?

Which area of passion would you be excited to pursue?

What will truly make you feel like you are "making a difference?"

In what direction do you feel drawn? What new ideas are coming to you?

Do you feel confident about your abilities?

○ YES   ○ NO   ○ SOMETIMES

What dream do you wish to manifest?

TRANSLATING VISION INTO REALITY

What step will you take in order to begin this manifesting journey?

Who do you need to contact?

What information do you need to move forward?

Where will you find it?

When will you begin?

How does you present dream relate to your Soul's purpose?

How, specifically, will you need to evolve in order to manifest your dream? Which personal characteristics will you choose to refine?

What can you do to stay conscious and aware of your own Precious Energy as well as any spiritual energy guiding and supporting you in manifesting your dream?

> "THE MORE I UNDERSTAND AND PERCEIVE, THE GREATER MY ABILITY TO MAKE MY DREAMS AND DESTINY COME TRUE."
>
> —*MANIFESTING YOU DREAMS*
> By Bonnie Barness

SPIRITUAL PATH

SUPPLEMENTAL READING: *EXPERIENCING THE SHIFT* BY BONNIE BARNESS

Your Soul has come to Earth in order to evolve and refine specific characteristics. Through the Soul's Lens, you will begin to see how situations are created for that exact purpose. As you go through each situation, you will begin to ask yourself the following questions, "Is there a spiritual lesson to be learned? Is this related to my life's purpose? Is there something greater than myself supporting and guiding me during this time? Is my True Self being reflected in each and every one of my actions? What opportunity for spiritual growth is present in the situation?

Going through life, thinking, seeing, and being in a new way, will give you the opportunity to evolve at a much faster rate. Sometimes life circumstances will be filled with joy, unexpected surprises and fun. At other times, they will be filled with pain and loss. Looking at situations from the higher vantage point of the Soul, will allow you to transform each experience into a much deeper one. Feelings of joy can grow while feelings of pain can lessen.

You, your Soul, contains an abundance of gifts and talents. These are yours, your own unique beauty that is to be shared with the world. They are the gifts needed to fulfill your Soul's purpose. Follow your heart and pursue what you love. Take actions that are meaningful to you and make you feel that the time you have here on Earth is being used to make a difference in the live of others.

As you move forward on your new path, look at the possibilities that present themselves to you.. Take action and listen to your heart and Soul. Feel your vibration and watch as the frequency increases as you connect more deeply and profoundly with your True Self and your life's purpose.

As you move forward on your manifesting path, are you receiving a positive response from the people you have contacted?

◯ YES   ◯ NO

Are you gaining useful information?

◯ YES   ◯ NO

Are doors opening or does it seem like obstacles arise at every turn?

_____
_____
_____

Are you "giving it your all?"

◯ YES   ◯ NO

Will you continue on this path?

◯ YES   ◯ NO

As doors open, how do you feel?

_____
_____
_____

SPIRITUAL PATH

What are the next steps you will take?

Having taken these steps, what has occurred?

If a new door has opened, what action will you take?

Are you open and receptive to new possibilities?

◯ YES   ◯ NO

If the doors have not opened, take time to reflect on how you feel and describe below.

From a spiritual vantage point, what message do you receive?

How have you grown, evolved, through this experience so far?

Are there different directions you can take in order to pursue your passion?

◯ YES   ◯ NO

Is there a different passion you wish to pursue?

SPIRITUAL PATH

SYNCHRONICITY AND COINCIDENCES

When your passion is in alignment with your destiny, often coincidences occur. Descibe below, any situations in which coincidences have occurred recently or in the past.

Synchronicity may also happen as you pursue your dream. Describe, below, any situations in which synchronicity has occurred presently or in the past.

As you proceed, are you meeting other people who are consciously involved in actualizing their Soul's purpose and pursuing their passion? Are people coming into your life who have information, skills, and talents essential to the fulfillment of your Soul's purpose? Are they conscious of their true purpose in your life? Describe below any special, spiritual interactions that have occurred.

Have you noticed that you are in partnership with something greater than yourself?

◯ YES ◯ NO

Are suprising and unexpected opportunities presenting themselves as you follow your passion? Describe below.

SPIRITUAL PATH

SPIRITUAL GROWTH OPPORTUNITIES

What are you learning from your new experiences?

WHAT CHALLENGES HAVE ARISEN? WHAT RESISTANCE HAVE YOU EXPERIENCED?

Intellectually

Emotionally

Physically

Spiritually

Psychologically

Life Skills

Which of these challenges and areas of resistance have occurred in the past?

What spiritual lesson and opportunities for growth can be gained from these experiences?

Have these new situations given you an opportunity to grow by,
- Developing more inner control
- Gaining more insight into other people
- Gaining more insight into yourself
- Utilizing knowledge acquired
- Giving to others
- Receiving from others

How have you stayed connected to your True Self throughout the process?

How have you sustained focus, effort and concentration while using your Precious Energy consistently in the manifesting process? Describe below.

_____
_____
_____
_____

What activities can add to your life to release stress and stay in balance?

_____
_____
_____

Are you able to distinguish between your personal thoughts and desires and your Soul's longing?

○ YES   ○ NO

Are you filled with gratitude for the opportunity to pursue your passion and purpose?

○ YES   ○ NO

Are you dealing effectively with your thoughts and feelings as they arise?

○ YES   ○ NO

Are you listening and allowing yourself to be guided by your Soul and your purpose versus listening to your Ego and your personal desires?

○ YES   ○ NO   ○ SOMETIMES

SPIRITUAL PATH

Are you treating yourself with respect?
◯ YES   ◯ NO   ◯ SOMETIMES

Are you aware of your expectations?
◯ YES   ◯ NO   ◯ SOMETIMES

Are you treating others with respect?
◯ YES   ◯ NO   ◯ SOMETIMES

Are you maintaining your integrity?
◯ YES   ◯ NO   ◯ SOMETIMES

Are you dealing effectively with life's realities?
◯ YES   ◯ NO   ◯ SOMETIMES

Are your actions in alignment with your True Self?
◯ YES   ◯ NO   ◯ SOMETIMES

Are you accepting of yourself versus being critical and judgmental?
◯ YES   ◯ NO   ◯ SOMETIMES

Are you accepting of others versus being critical and judgmental?
◯ YES   ◯ NO   ◯ SOMETIMES

Do you see the beauty within every person?
◯ YES   ◯ NO   ◯ SOMETIMES

Are you coming from a place of understanding with others?
◯ YES   ◯ NO   ◯ SOMETIMES

Do you appreciate your own uniqueness?
○ YES   ○ NO   ○ SOMETIMES

Are you looking at yourself through the Soul's Lens?
○ YES   ○ NO   ○ SOMETIMES

Are you filled with a sense of love for yourself and others?
○ YES   ○ NO   ○ SOMETIMES

Are you feeling the vibrational *SHIFT*?
○ YES   ○ NO   ○ SOMETIMES

Are you going through life with a new awareness of your thoughts, feelings and beliefs?
○ YES   ○ NO   ○ SOMETIMES

Are you consciously choosing your thoughts?
○ YES   ○ NO   ○ SOMETIMES

Are you feeling more excitement and passion for life?
○ YES   ○ NO   ○ SOMETIMES

NEW AWARENESS:

THE POWER TO CREATE

Have your manifesting actions made a difference in your life and the lives of others?

◯ YES ◯ NO

If they have, do you feel more fulfilled and have a greater sense of joy and peace?

◯ YES ◯ NO

Are you able to be completely "in the moment," totally present in each of your actions and interactions?

◯ YES ◯ NO

What have you manifested so far? How do you feel?

_____
_____
_____

What have you contributed to others?

_____
_____
_____

Have you been putting your well-being and connection to your True Self as you priority?

○ YES   ○ NO   ○ SOMETIMES

As you listen to your Soul, through this process, what new inspiration is emerging and flowing through you?

Where do you go from here?

Will you continue to move forward on this path?

○ YES   ○ NO

What new doors are waiting to be opened?

SPIRITUAL PATH

Are you already aware of what the next step is?

◯ YES ◯ NO

Do you have more clarity as to your purpose, your destiny?

◯ YES ◯ NO

Are you consciously partnering with the universe as you *SHIFT* into a new way of thinking, seeing and being?

◯ YES ◯ NO

Are you living in inspiration?

◯ YES ◯ NO

NEW AWARENESS:

EXPERIENCE THE SHIFT

Congratulations!

Through the steps you have taken on your new path, much wisdom and knowledge has been gained. You are connected more deeply and profoundly with your True Self, your Soul, your Essence than ever before in this lifetime. You are able to see more clearly who you truly are, the purpose of your life and your relationships. You can feel the spiritual energy flowing through you and all around you.

Experiencing the *SHIFT* into this higher level of consciousness is so exciting. As you continue on your incredible adventure, new insights and Truths will be revealed. More of your True Self will be reflected in the world as you evolve through lessons learned. Great spiritual knowledge will become known. In time, you will experience other *SHIFTS* in consciousness. With each *SHIFT*, you will access more of your Soul—your gifts, talents, inner wisdom—and the spiritual realm.

Know that you are here for a reason. You have a purpose that is uniquely yours. Connected to your True Self, to your Soul, and to the universal spiritual energy, you are now more consciously involved in the actualization of your True Self and in the fulfillment of your Soul's purpose. You are a blessing. Let your beauty shine for all to experience.

It is my honor to be by your side as you move forward on your life's journey!

Bonnie Barness

ABOUT THE AUTHOR

Bonnie Barness is from Beverly Hills, California and is a graduate of U.C.L.A. She currently resides in Scottsdale, Arizona, where she maintains a private practice providing psychotherapy, hypnotherapy, and life coaching.

Ms. Barness has created a process in which individuals are able to shift out of pain, blocks, barriers, and limitations into a new state of consciousness, allowing for a greater experience of joy, happiness, fulfillment and the manifestation of dreams. This method, the Barness SHIFT Method, provides hope, relief and freedom for individuals of all ages dealing with anxiety, depression, loss and addiction. She helps couples and families move out of conflict into deep intimate connections. Those consciously on a spiritual path reach new levels of insight, understanding and experience. For some, the SHIFT takes place over a period of time. For others, it happens immediately.

As an author and speaker, Ms. Barness enjoys sharing her unique approach to life, relationships and spiritual growth with others. On radio and television, as an expert source for the Arizona Republic and in her advice column, "Ask Bonnie", she has provided specific strategies for dealing with life's challenges and for living life to its fullest.

Through her books and workbooks, **Finding the Balance, Experiencing the Shift, Manifesting Your Dreams, Emotional Intelligence, The Soul's Lens, Freedom from Addiction**, as well as during SHIFT workshops, SHIFT weekend retreats and the SHIFT AP Tele-Seminars, she supports individuals of all ages make dreams into reality. For more information about her books and events, please visit BonnieBarness.com. If you are interested in arranging future speaking engagements and private events or sessions, please email her at Bonnie@BonnieBarness.com.

www.ingramcontent.com/pod-product-compliance
Lightning Source LLC
Chambersburg PA
CBHW060530010526
44110CB00052B/2554